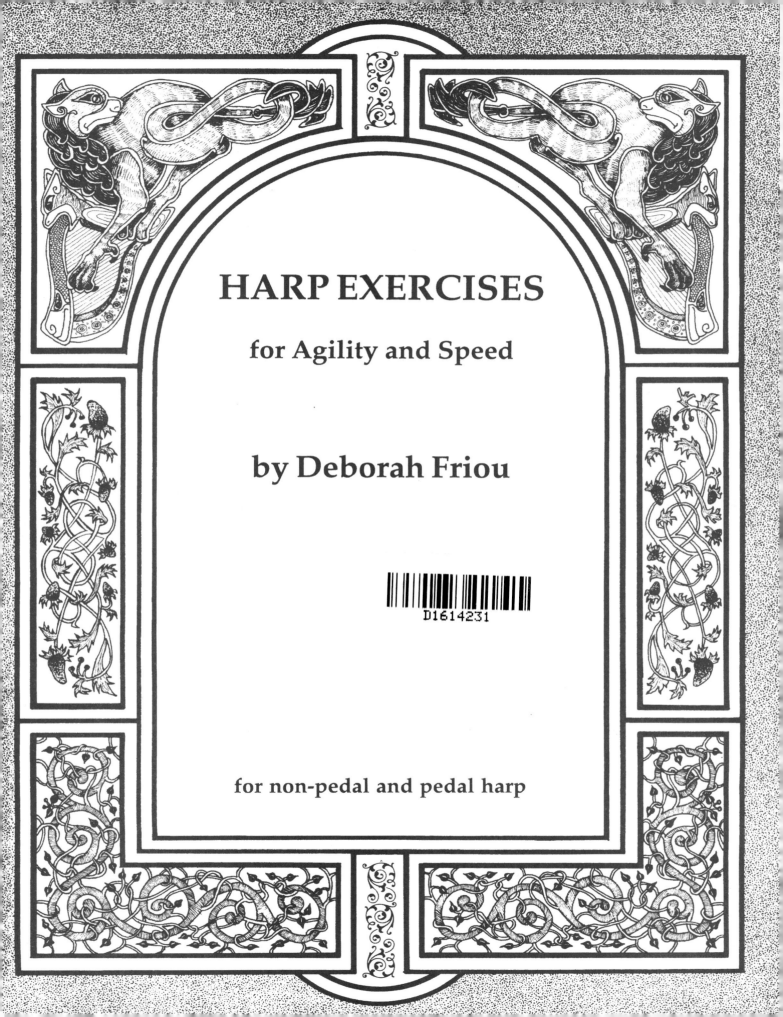

HARP EXERCISES

for Agility and Speed

by Deborah Friou

for non-pedal and pedal harp

Cover art by **Linda Friou**

© 1989 by Deborah Friou
Friou Music
P.O. Box 157
Brunswick, ME 04011
U.S.A.

ISBN 978-0-9628120-3-3

INTRODUCTION

This book was designed to help harp players develop and maintain strength, suppleness, and agility in the fingers and hands. It is intended for use by players of all levels. The repetition of patterns common to the harp should enable the player to perform with greater ease and confidence.

A few pieces of music have been included where additional practice of the skills involved seemed helpful. The exercises are arranged in a rough sequential order, however, you will proabably wish to skip around in the book. The pieces, exercises and etudes are in the key of C tuning with only one exception which requires one sharp.

Beginners should be sure to start out playing one hand at a time in the exercises which combine two staves.

Relaxation is very important. Pause between exercises, shake the hands out, especially when playing the more complex scales and four-finger patterns. Remember that you're striving to increase agility as well as strength and speed. Also be sure to keep your playing at an even tempo. Play at a speed at which it is possible to maintain this.

Exercises are great for warming up, varying your practice, and moving your playing to a new plateau. We hope you get much good use from this book.

CONTENTS

I. TWO NOTE CHORDS

Both fingers should sound together and be of equal strength.

Scales

Fingers should pluck into palm.

Exercises With Two Note Chords

Practice hands separately first.

Thirds

2

Sixths   Second finger should hang down rather than curling up.

4

Combining Intervals

Twll Yn Ei Boch

Welsh

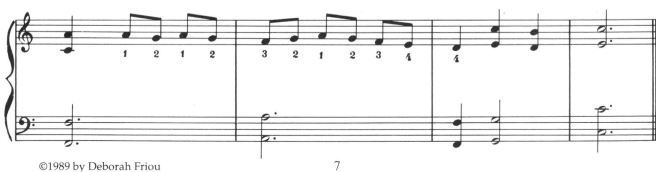

7

Annie Laurie

Scottish

II. TWO FINGER EXERCISES

Replace firmly to avoid buzzing.

Practice hands separately first.

III. THREE FINGER EXERCISES

Place 3 fingers together.   Keep thumb pointing up.

11

Practice hands separately first.

14

IV. TRIADS AND INVERSIONS

Place 3 fingers together.

16

Key of C Major Triads and Inversions Two Hands

Fingers should close in a relaxed fashion into the hand.

Fine

D.C. al
Fine

17

Descending Triads

Left Hand

Fine

L.H.

L.H.

L.H.

L.H.

L.H.

D.C. al Fine

18

Exercises with Triads and Inversions

Listen for a smooth transition between the two hands.

Etude

24

V. FOUR FINGER EXERCISES

25

Practice hands separately first.

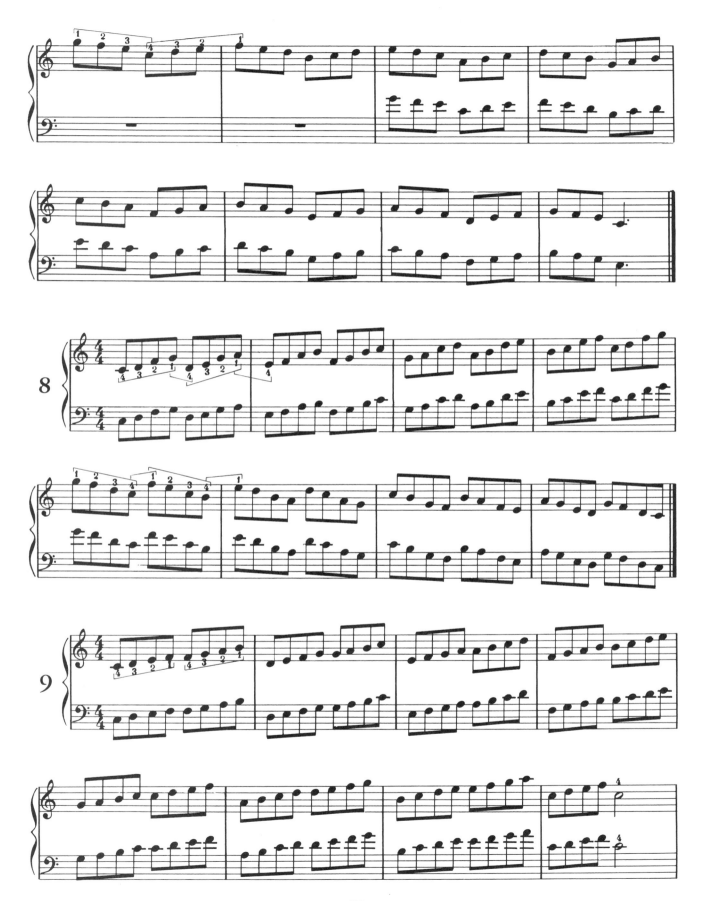

VI.PLAYING WITHOUT THE THUMB

VII. 4-2-1 PATTERNS

32

VIII. FOUR FINGER ARPEGGIOS

Close fingers into palm.

Arpeggios in the Key of C Major

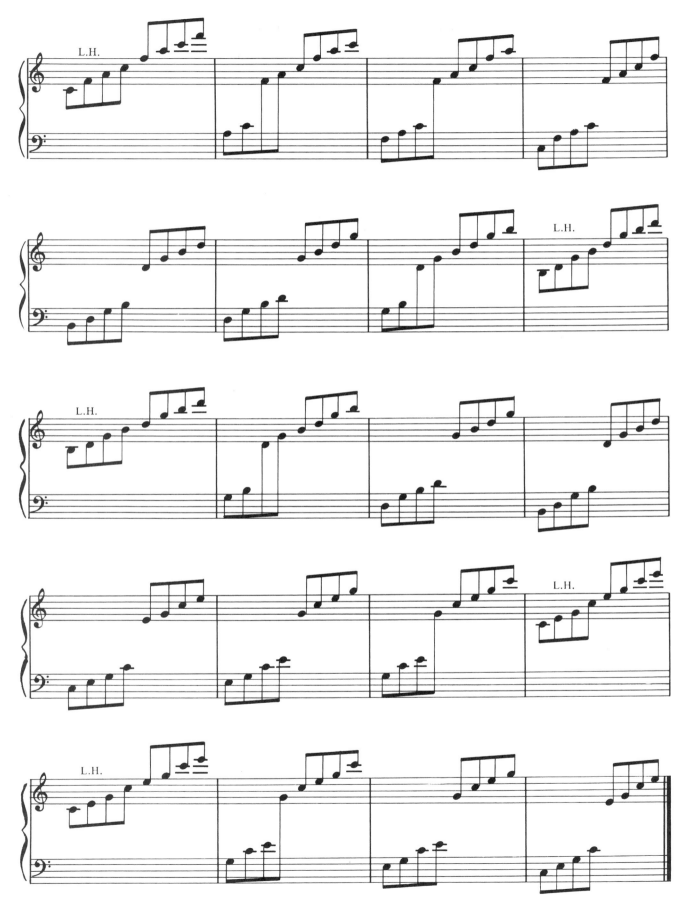

34

Descending Arpeggios

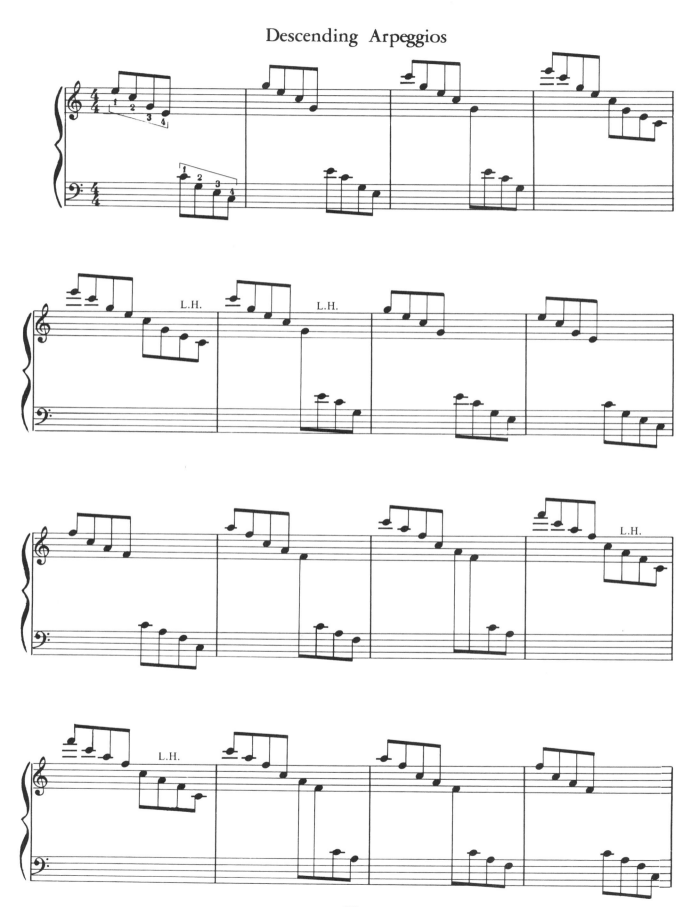

35

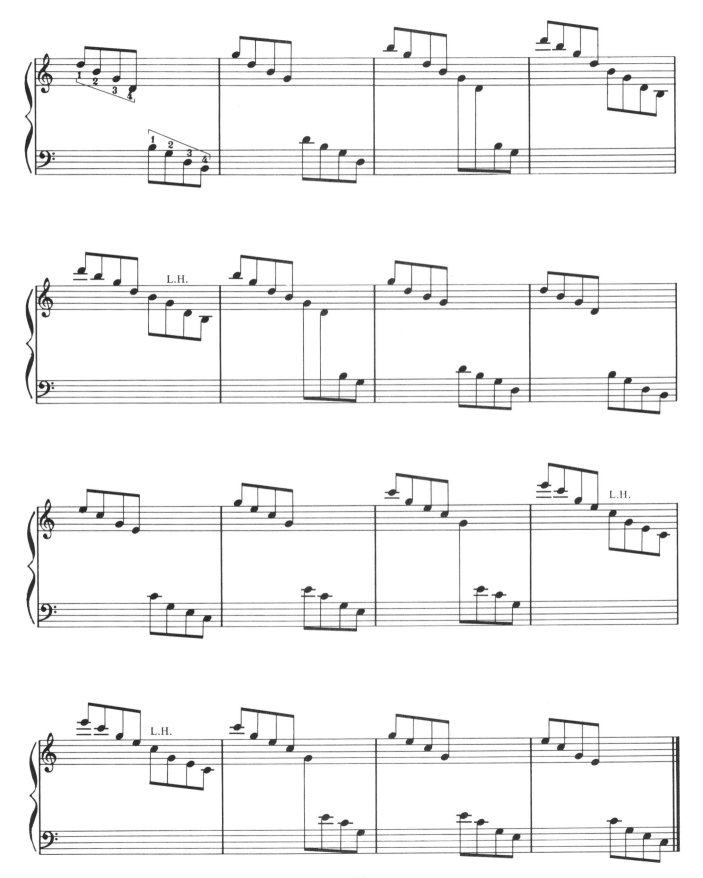

Arpeggios in the Key of A Minor

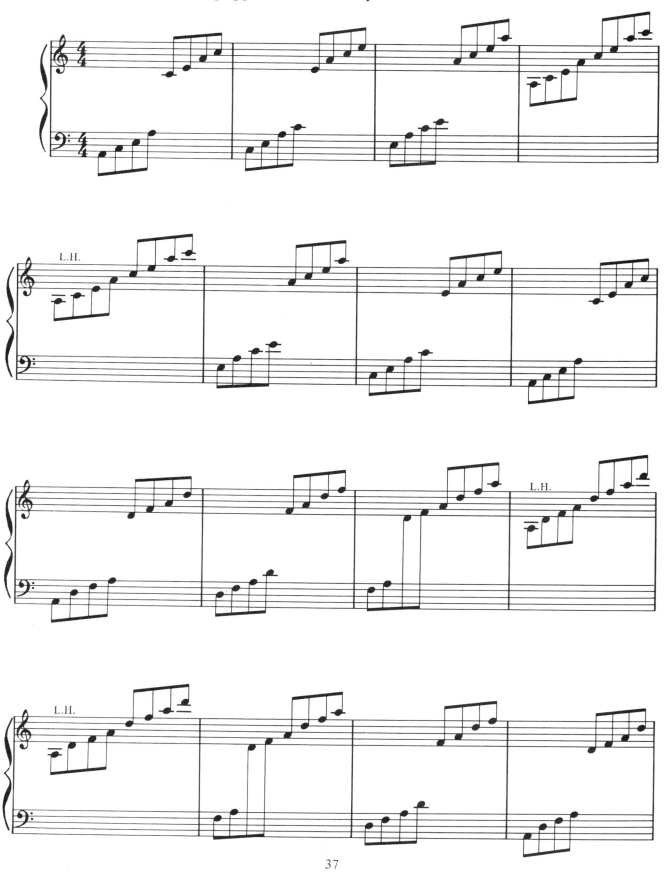

37

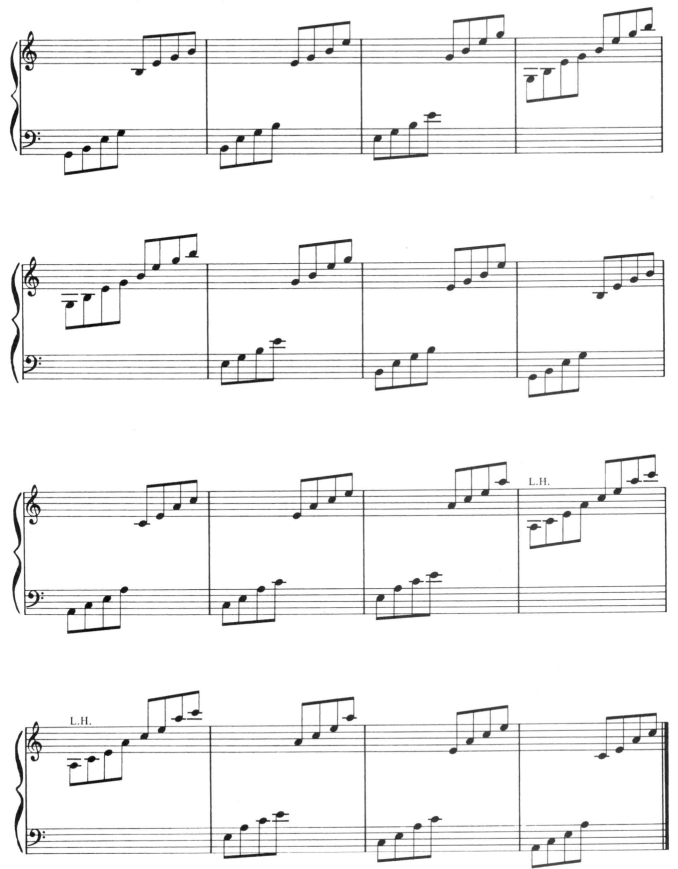

38

Arpeggio Exercises

44

More Arpeggio Exercises

1

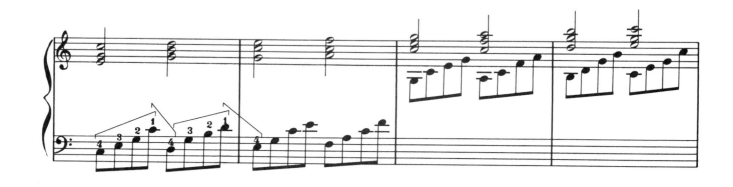

Overlapping Arpeggios Right Hand

Overlapping Arpeggios Left Hand

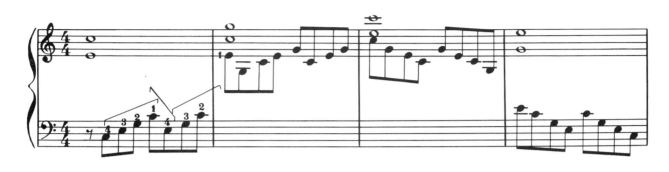

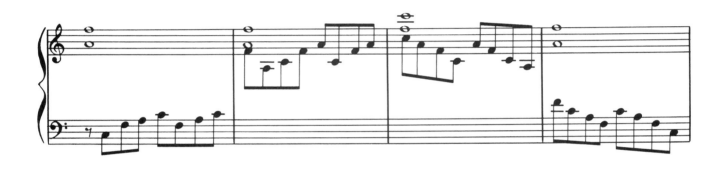

IX. ROLLED CHORDS

Three Finger Chords

Practice for evenness and speed.

Notes in parentheses should be placed.
The finger will then remain on the string.

Chords of three or more notes will be rolled.

Right Hand

Close fingers into palm.

Left Hand

Rolled Chords With Two Hands

Listen for a smooth transition between the two hands.

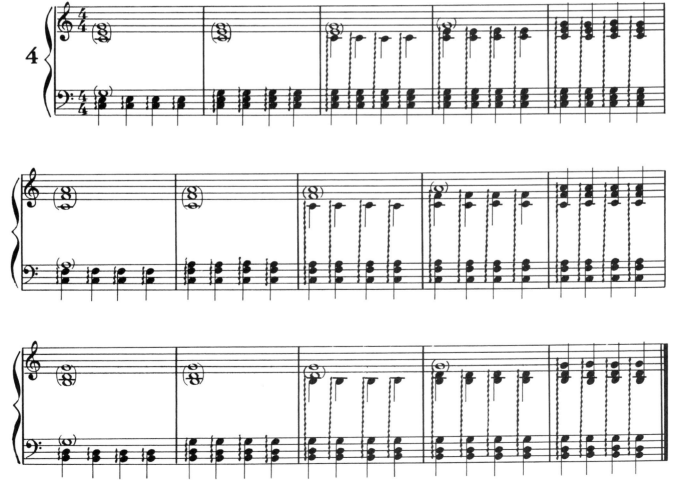

The Trees They Do Grow High

English

Four Finger Chords

Notes in parentheses should be placed. The finger will then remain on the string.

Notes in parentheses should be placed.
The finger will then remain on the string.

4 Finger Chords-Two Hands

Close fingers into palm.

Mwynen Ceiriog

Welsh

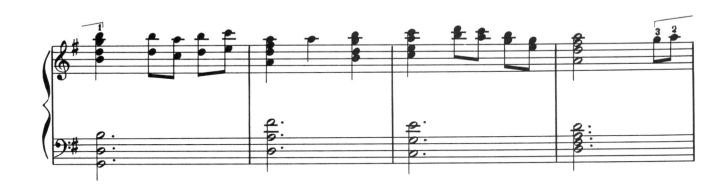

Playing Chords and Single Notes

Rolling Chords and Double Notes

X. SLIDES

Thumb Slides

Isolate the thumb to execute a slide.   Practice hands separately first.

Fourth Finger Slides

Slides With Chords

Right Hand

Left Hand

Exercises With Slides

XI. CROSS-OVERS and CROSS-UNDERS

Preparation for Cross-Overs

Practice hands separately first.

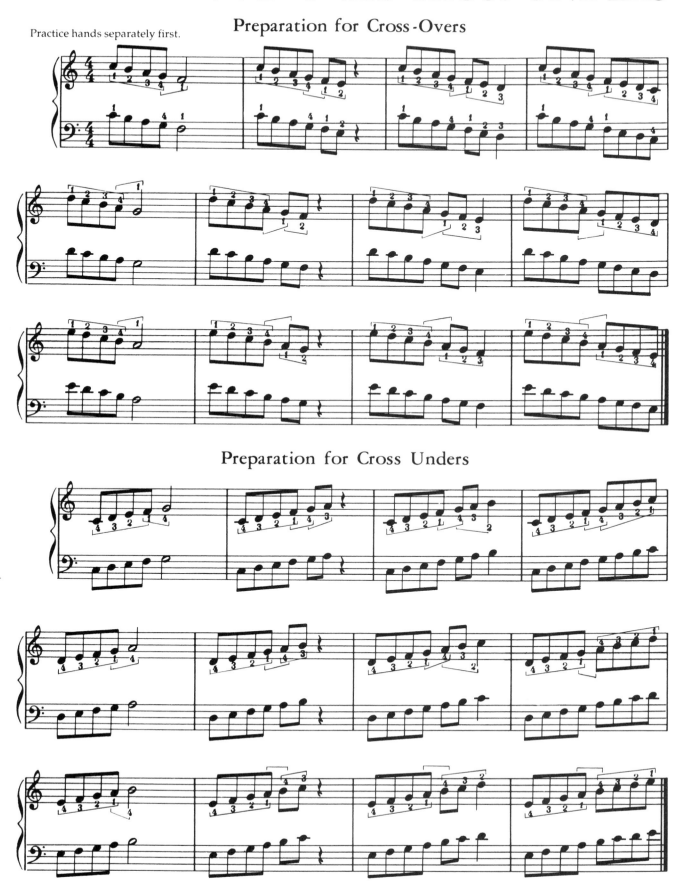

Preparation for Cross Unders

One Octave Scales

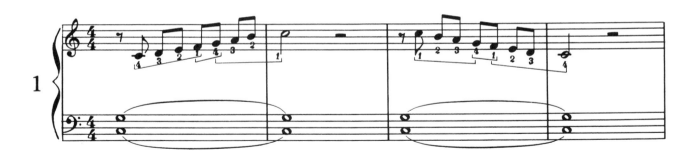

1

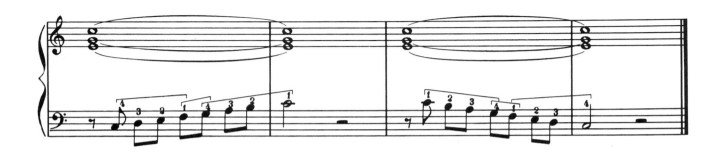

2

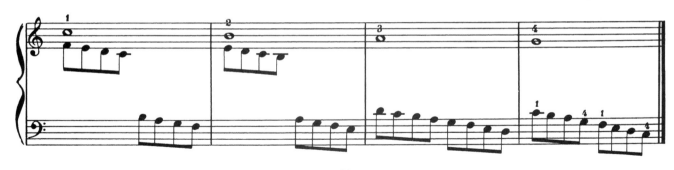

Practice right hand separately first.

5

Practice left hand separately first.

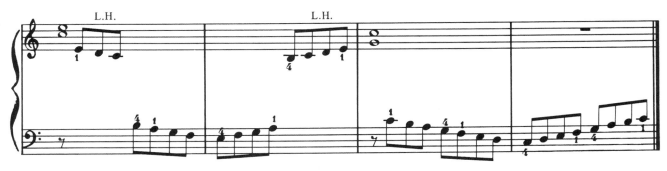

Exercises for Crossing Under the Fourth Finger

Exercises for Crossing Over the Thumb

Scales With the Third Finger Crossing

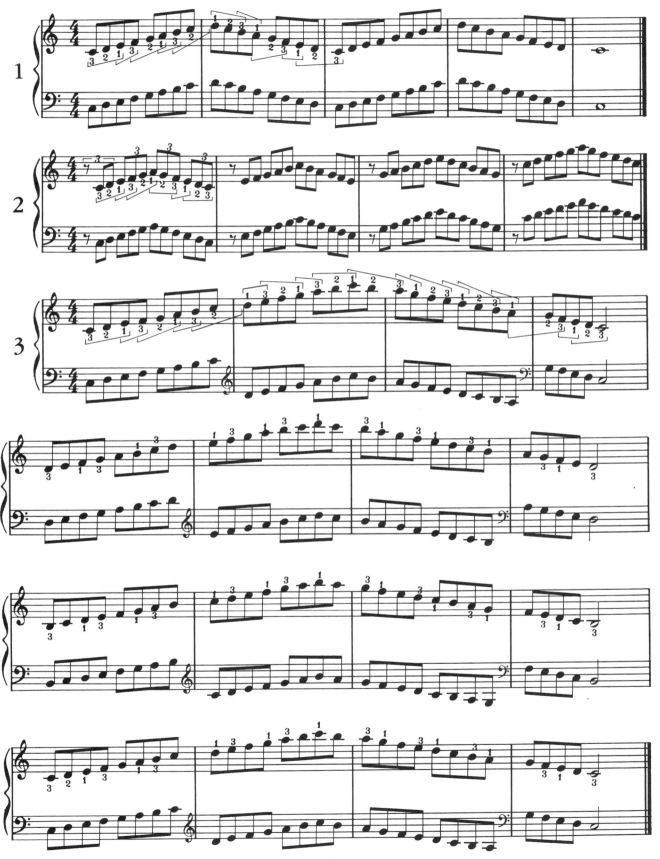

Extended Scales

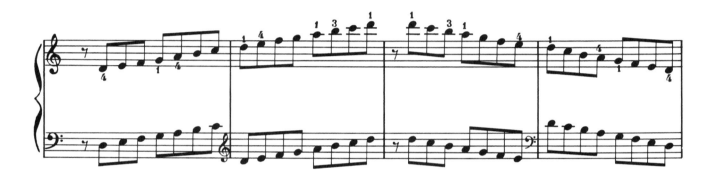

Practice hands separately first.

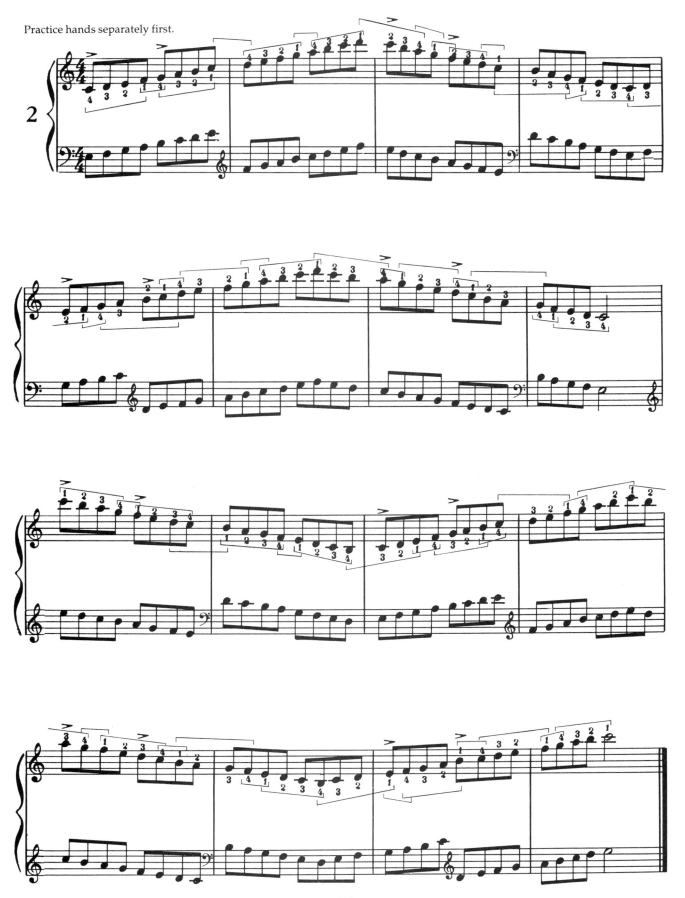

More Scales

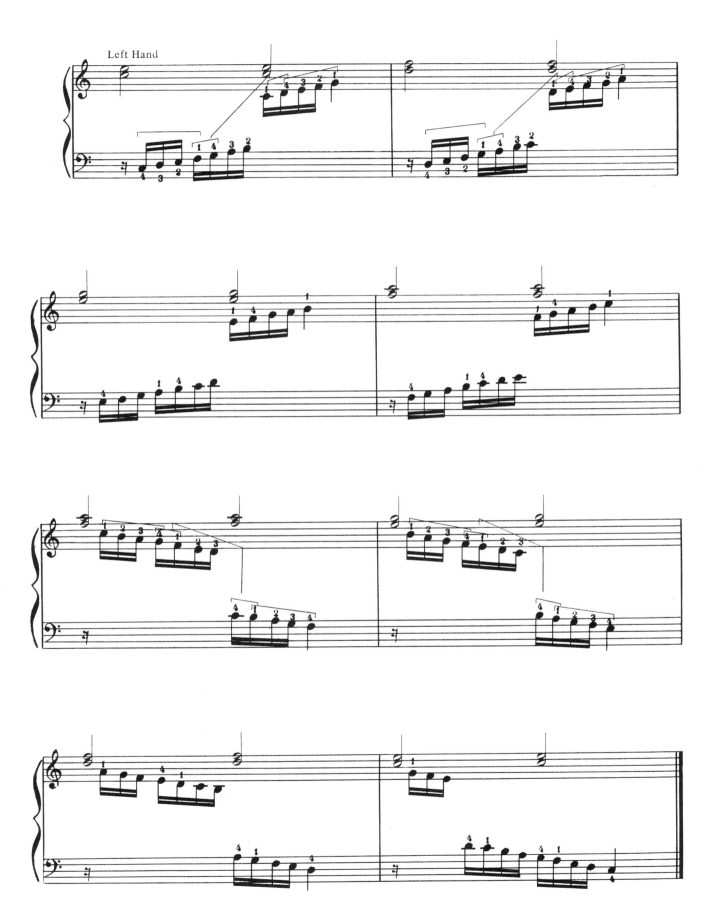

Scales with the Second Finger Crossing

Exercises With Cross-Overs and Unders

Cross-Over Arpeggios

XII. JUMPS

The following exercises should be done with each of the four fingers, one at a time.

XIII.FINGER INDEPENDENCE

Notes in parentheses should be placed.
The finger will then remain on the string.

Strengthening Individual Fingers

Strengthening Third and Fourth Fingers

Improving Finger Independence

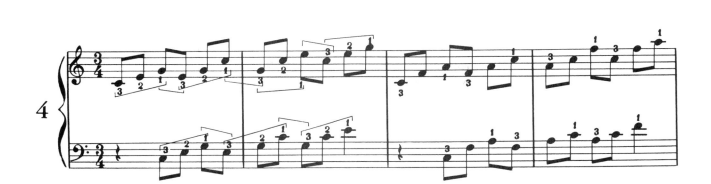

XIV. THEME AND VARIATIONS

Theme

Welsh

89

Var. 6